Stefan Grossman's Guitar Workshop Audio Series

MW00562022

John Renbourn
Fingerstyle Guitar

Folk, Blues & Beyond, Celtic Melodies & Open Tunings, and The Jazz Tinge

The audio recordings available online are taken from John Renbourn's video lessons of the same titles.

Online Audio   www.melbay.com/98511MEB

Visit us at www.melbay.com — E-mail us at email@melbay.com

Primrose Hill, London, England 1974

Photo by Roger Perry

Contents

FOLK, BLUES & BEYOND

CELTIC MELODIES & OPEN TUNINGS

THE JAZZ TINGE

John Renbourn discusses the tunes
in this collection with Stefan Grossman

STEFAN: Let's begin by talking about the tunes presented in your *Folk, Blues & Beyond* lesson.

JOHN: *Judy* is a piece of mock medieval minimalism. I play a back beat in 3/4 and fool around with this little syncopated pattern.

STEFAN: *Angie?*

JOHN: *Angie* is a Davey Graham tune. I put together bits and pieces of that back in the early 1960s while I was travelling around. I met lots of other guitar players who played bits and pieces of that instrumental. Most had learned it from an EP that Davey recorded with Alexis Korner.

STEFAN: *Watch The Stars?*

JOHN: *Watch The Stars* is also one that I picked up around about that time. I heard that it was an American traditional song, a children's song. Peggy Seeger used to sing it when she was in England but I actually heard it from a guy named Barry Thomas who, I think, used to play occasionally with Peggy. I changed it around and came up with my version in the key of A.

STEFAN: *Lord Franklin?*

JOHN: *Lord Franklin* is a very well established British ballad about Sir John Franklin's expedition to find a trade route to the East, in I think the 1830s. There were a number of good version around the folk scene before I figured mine out. Martin Carthy played a good version in D. I remember being down on a beach in North Africa in the 1960s, playing that tune and working it out in E. The same tune for *Lord Franklin* is one that's done the rounds and is used for a song called *McCafferty*. That is a kind of anti-army song.

STEFAN: Now for something completely different: *My Sweet Potato.*

JOHN: This is a piece from a Booker T. and the MGs album titled *Time Is Tight.* It's probably not one of their better known albums but it came from the period after they made *Green Onion* and all those good tunes.

STEFAN: And what got you into arranging a rock n'roll tune ?

JOHN: I used to play rock in the band *Hooksnort Rupert And His Famous Porkchestra* before I started to play on the folk scene. That's where I got the 3/4 back beat and stuff like that. This particular Booker T. tune is really nice because it's just got him playing with Duck Dunn on bass and Al Jackson on drums. Booker T. plays the electric piano. What I like about this type of tune is that it has parts and a steady bass with a top line. It's really pretty.

STEFAN: How about the hymn *Abide With Me?*

JOHN: *Abide With Me* is really one of the best known Victorian hymn tunes by a composer called Monk. The story is that it's associated with Brixham, which is the next village down from where I live in the West Country. It's a particularly strong four part hymn tune and a nice one.

STEFAN: From what period of time?

JOHN: Victorian I guess. It's in most of the old hymn books.

STEFAN: Where did you hear *Great Dreams From Heaven?*

JOHN: *Great Dreams From Heaven* is a tune from Joseph Spence, the Bahamian guitar player and singer. I guess it is also an adaption of a hymn tune. There are a great many songs that are attached to this melody - one is *The Masters Bouquet*, a very nice early bluegrass song that the Stanley Brothers recorded. There are others that I can't remember. Jean Ritchie sang me a few that were the same tune for example, so Spence must have adapted the tune and put a really nice guitar part to it. I've taken that and when I perform I blend *Abide With Me* and *Great Dreams From Heaven* in a medley.

STEFAN: Let's talk about the tunes in the your second lesson CD: *Celtic Melodies and Open Tunings*. Let's start with *The South Wind*.

JOHN: *The South Wind* is one of the best known slow aires from West Clare, down in the west of Ireland. I've heard it played an awful lot there and in other places. I remember it being played by the great uileean piper Willy Clancy when I was over in Ireland in the 1960s and the tune has done the rounds. I've also heard a lot of guitar players do it. My version seems to sit nicely in D. I retune the sixth and first strings down to D.

STEFAN: What is the challenge in arranging an aire pipe tune on the guitar?

JOHN: Well they all vary slightly. The pipe tunes often have some very nice ornamentations. To be honest, I wouldn't say I put in too much in that particular tune but the challenge is really to make it sustain and hold and be a real solid piece.

STEFAN: And you're playing that in what tuning?

JOHN: D down: D A D G B D.

STEFAN: Let's talk about *The Blarney Pilgrim*.

JOHN: I heard a nice version of *The Blarney Pilgrim* from Paul Brady. He played it on the mandolin. I've heard it before and since by many traditional players. It's one of the standard jigs/fiddle tunes and a nice one with three sections.

STEFAN: What's the challenge of trying to play a very rhythmic Irish dance tune on the guitar?

JOHN: There are a lot of arrangements of traditional tunes and often they sound like parlor or party pieces when they're played. Usually they're played fingerstyle on a nylon strung guitar in standard tuning and they're transferred from being what originally they were, which is a piece of music to dance to, to being a piece to simply listen to. It doesn't have to have the kick and it doesn't have to make you want to dance but if you can do that then you've achieved really what the music is all about.

STEFAN: And the tuning that you use for The *Blarney Pilgrim* ?

JOHN: That one works in open G (D G D G B D). I like to combine *The South Wind* (played in D A D G B D) with *The Blarney Pilgrim*. Towards the end of *The South Wind* I have to change the 5th string by dropping it down a tone. I do that by playing a harmonic and try to retune it to a G. *The Blarney Pilgrim* is played in the key of D (though in an open G tuning) and for some reason I wound up with that G string there because I wanted to have a nice ascending bass coming up across the line towards the end of the tune.

Stefan: So you're in an open G tuning but you're playing in the key of D.

JOHN: Yes

STEFAN: How about *Bunyan's Hymn*?

JOHN: Well, like *Abide With Me*, *Bunyan's Hymn* is a very well known English hymn tune, which is associated with John Bunyan because the words are all about being a pilgrim. It's a very strong major keyed tune with a nice melody and harmonic strength. But it seems that the original tune was a folk tune and was about a blacksmith and nothing to do with being a pilgrim at all, quite different.

STEFAN: And what tuning are you playing that in?

JOHN: It's in open G and most of the tune fits really nicely in that tuning (D G D G B D).

STEFAN: And how did you come to set it in Open G. Did you experiment or did you just feel that that would be the right tuning.

JOHN: With a number of these arrangements I've just been fooling around looking at hymn books and reading the piano parts. With *Abide With Me* I don't think I sat down and worked it out on the guitar, I had the parts memorized because I'd learnt the tune simply to find out how the parts were worked. So then once I'd got an idea of how you approached the harmonization I found I couldn't resist playing them on the guitar and it fitted OK in D. It probably fits in may other keys as well. And the same thing with *Bunyan's Hymn*. I tackled that because I liked the melody and the time changes in it and I kind of reharmonized it to fit in open G deliberately.

STEFAN: How about *I Saw Three Ships?*

JOHN: *I Saw Three Ships* is also a traditional English tune and a very charming one. It's very simple but it seems to have great appeal. I really like the tune and I know a lot of other people that have a great fondness for it. It seems to me to be a really old tune, I can't say how old but it could easily fit in with the concept of medieval dance tunes that I've come across without very much change and it flows very nicely. It has a little refrain to it and that also fits very nicely in that same tuning. So I play the two together and I throw in an number of other tradition English tunes in that medley.

STEFAN: How did you find *The English Dance?*

JOHN: Well I think I must have heard that also a long time ago being played by a man named Francis Bain, who was involved pretty early on in the revival of early music. He was before David Monroe. Before the kind of better, more wide spread groups that specialized in early music. I think I liked *The English Dance* because it features a repetitive melodic tune in a major key. I think the instrument that Francis Bain played was the fiddelle which was an old type of bowed instrument larger than a violi. *The English Dance* has a real punch to it when it's played on a bowed instrument because you can get top string drones against the descending patterns and I happen to like that. I found that it fitted nicely on the guitar in the open G tuning.

STEFAN: On stage you joke that it's one of the few English dances from that period of English music.

JOHN; Well, there have been quite a lot of manuscripts supposedly of English music. Lots are lodged in The British Museum but how many of them are actually English manuscripts to start, with I don't know. I think in fact, a great deal of the early dance tunes are probably northern Italian, but I think there is a chance that this one is English. Not that it matters a great deal but there we are you know – there's a certain national pride I suppose.

STEFAN: Let's talk about how you found the open G minor tuning that you use for several Celtic melodies.

JOHN: OK. There were quite a selection of tunings in the G group that were handy. I used to often use a tuning with the second string up to C which meant if I was playing medieval dance tunes – I used to play a tune called *Trotto* and another titled *Salterello* that both fitted quite nicely in that tuning – you could play low drones and still keep the melody going. The G minor tuning is just a variation: the second string tuned to the minor third rather than the 4th or the 2nd or whichever you like. I can't remember what I first used it for. I have an arrangement of *The Moon Shines Bright* which is quite a long elaborate piece. This uses the tuning and later on I used it for *Nine Maidens*.

STEFAN: Where did you find *Owen Roe O'Neill?*

JOHN: *Owen Roe O'Neill* is noted in the O'Neal's collection under the Carolan tunes and I wouldn't be surprised if it in Bunting's as well. In fact, I think it's in Bunting's with a harmonization by Bunting, but I took mine from the top line and harmonized it. It fits pretty nicely on the guitar in the open G minor tuning.

STEFAN: And *Mist Covered Mountains Of Home ?*

JOHN: *Mist Covered Mountains Of Home* is a tune I learned from a fiddle player who I think got it from Jody Stecher. It's a highland pipe tune and it's an unusual one. Someone some time back sent me a harmony part for a second bagpipe part. I don't know of many tunes that have two bagpipes in close harmony but apparently this one has been arranged that way. I've always imagined that it's was a song but I've never actually heard complete verses sung to it.

6

STEFAN: And *The Orphan?*

JOHN: I learned that from Dougie McLean and I have the feeling that that's an Irish tune. I try to get in some of the turns, the crans and the burls that pipers and fiddle players use.

STEFAN: When you play all three of those tunes in a set your right hand technique changes quite dramatically from one song to another - do you want to talk a little bit about that?

JOHN: Well only that they're three quite different type of pieces. The first one is a lament which should be slow and harp like so the right hand technique features very slow arpeggios. With *Mist Covered Mountains of Home* I generally have that arranged so the tune is in the bass and my three fingers play on the treble strings (playing an arpeggio pattern on the treble strings) with the thumb holding the low melody. *The Orphan* is played with a damped bass against a top line which is the jig line with the decorations. So yes, I use three separate right hand styles.

STEFAN: Does the influence of the Celtic harp have anything to do with your approach in playing guitar arrangements of Celtic music.

JOHN: Well it's like an imagined influence more than a real one. The Celtic Harp did die out quite drastically. I think Bunting's idea was to try to preserve music the old harpers, and there weren't many left even then back in the 1700s. It is interesting to imagine how the tradition would have been. What has survived from the old harp music that we know of has become keyboard music or gone into the pipes or gone into the fiddle. But the tunes give you clues that they were originally played on the harp. But what's intriguing of course, is that the old harp would have been metal strung and this throws out quite a few questions. The harp tuning would have been diatonic. We guess probably without semi tone tuning levers. So the whole subject is quite interesting.

STEFAN: How does that effect your right hand technique?

JOHN: Only that the technique that I've always used has been the thumb and three fingers. So there's no

Milano, Italy 1973

Photo by Guido Harari

7

other technique that I really think about. I limit my playing sometimes for some types of music but normally I use what I consider to be the classical technique. I would imagine that harpers would have played like that as well.

STEFAN: What I'm try to get at is that that type of guitar playing is very European – very British – as far as the accenting and the right hand approach. An American musician wouldn't play instinctively that way.

JOHN: I think what's happened with the British stuff is there was no on going folk tradition on the guitar at all. In America people have inherited set techniques which are absolutely very well defined. There's the flatpick technique and there's the thumbstyle and one finger technique and so on. These things didn't exist in England so the people that came to the guitar often came through a general classical, for want of a better word, approach and then took up the steel string guitar often against advise from their so called betters. They found that this approach worked for steel strings, it opened up a lot more possibilities. I would think it would be very difficult to play a flowing harp tune using only a thumb pick and index finger.

STEFAN: *Lindsay?*

JOHN: Archie Fisher was one of the biggest early influences on the British guitar players along with Davey Graham. Archie's influence was stronger from the traditional standpoint. His playing is wonderful and this particular song is one of his own songs. It's from a record I think called *Will Ye Gang* . I think it's a Topic Record, a fairly early one. The tune has a very nice traditional feel to it and I preface the song with a slow aire which is called *Tramps And Hawkers*. This has been one of the perennial Scottish traditional songs, a very nice one with a very nice set of words. The melody has been used for a number of other songs. Bob Dylan took it for *I Pity The Poor Immigrant* and I've heard it quite a few times for other songs as well.

STEFAN: How about *Sandwood Down To Kyle?*

JOHN: I heard snatches of *Sandwood Down To Kyle* from Dougie McLean while I was traveling around with him. It had a very haunting melody and it stayed with me for a long time. So long in fact, I wished I could find the remainder of the tune and one day I phoned Duncan McClennen, who is a fine singer and used to run the Inverness Club and festival, and on the spur of the moment asked him did he know it and I sang him a few snatches and he completed it for me. So I found the rest of the song and it turned out to be one of Dave Goulder's songs and not surprisingly it's wonderful. Dave wrote *The January Man* and quite a few other tunes. *Sandwood Down To Kyle* fits nicely in the same tuning that I do *Lindsay* which is DADGAD.

STEFAN: Let's talk about the instrumentals featured on *The Jazz Tinge* lesson. You begin with *Buffalo*. This is back to normal tuning ?

JOHN: Yes *Buffalo* is back in A. I heard bits and pieces of this from other people when I was knocking around at the same time as I heard *Angie*. I mean I met all kinds of guitar players back in the very early 1960s. So that particular tune turned out to be by Davey Graham. Atleast the head is by Davey. He was playing in parallel 6ths, perhaps I mentioned this on the lesson. The whole piece is based around these intervals. It's a kind of minor keyed blues sequence. Davey mentioned he used to listen to piano players such as Horace Silver, he liked him very much, and when I came to record early on I used that as a vehicle just to play blues in A which I already played quite a fair amount of. So it's a combination of the idea of using purely 6ths in a minor key blues and playing around a blues sequence.

STEFAN: How about *Transfusion?*

JOHN: This is a tune from a record by Chico Hamilton that featured Charles Lloyd. Charles Lloyd later went on to write a number of really nice pieces. Chico Hamilton and Charles Lloyd were quite a big influence on guys like myself, Davey and Bert, who were sitting around listening to music other than traditional folk music. There was a record called *Passing Through* which we liked very much and I think that track *Transfusion* came from that record. What was appealing about it was those groups, Charles Lloyd's, Chico Hamilton's, John Handy's, Charlies Mingus, a lot of bands of that type were using horns and the rest of the instruments not simply as solo and rhythm sections but as a kind of an integrated counterpoint and this was the appeal of that music.

STEFAN: *My Dear Boy?*

JOHN: Some of the fun of this music is to play lines against moving lines. *My Dear Boy* has a bass pattern that goes up and a top line that goes down. There are hundreds and hundreds of tunes that use this same idea and I can't remember if I based mine on anything imparticular. I don't think I did. I think I just took it and found these parts worked rather nicely on the guitar. It's again an extension of playing what I consider to be a traditional blues in A.

STEFAN: *Little Niles?*

JOHN: I heard the tune *Little Niles* when Duck Baker came to my house with a big pile of records which included a lot of piano players that he wanted us to listen to. One was Dollar Brand and the other was Randy Weston. There were quite a number of them that were really good. We listened to these guys and it was fantastic. Of a number of tunes that stood out *Little Niles* was very attractive, so I tried to work out an arrangement. In fact again, I didn't really sit down and work out an arrangement like the hymn tunes, I thought about what was happening in the music and what the chords were and how the piece was constructed and later on found that it could turn out pretty nicely on the guitar. I based my guitar arrangement on Dollar Brand's recording of the tune that was written by Randy Weston.

STEFAN: And did you first play it on the piano or right away on the guitar ?

JOHN: I kind of fooled around a little bit on the piano to see what was happening with the time and the chords and what was happening with the parts. It's a very well constructed tune and once you see what's happening with the lines, you can see how the thinking goes behind it.

STEFAN: What's happening with the lines? What's the thinking behind it?

JOHN: First of all it's in a slow three and there's two notes in my opinion which sort of hold the tune together over two chords. One is the third and if you're in A minor that's C natural and if you go change to the D9 chord you make it a modal chord. It's F sharp. So that would be the major third of the D. So this is actually just a key little phrase but it's very pretty but it more or less sets the tone of the melody. The melody starts by running up to the C and then you have the F sharp coming in to the bass and the chord changes. Then it completes the sequence by going down chromatically so you have an F9 descending to a dominant E chord but with a flat 9 on the top. So it's just a very pretty little figure and this is the way the tune got its hook to start off with and then he extends that idea and adds two different sections to it and then improvises around the middle – basically around those two chords and those two notes.

STEFAN: And lastly, let's talk about *Cherry*.

JOHN: *Cherry* is a tune from Dollar Brand. There are a great many tunes that he wrote that have got a really nice African District 6 rhythmic feel to it. District 6 is the area in Cape Town where he came from that produced a lot of music that's a combination of church music and African rhythm music. It's really swings along nicely. I like *Cherry* because it fits those two things: it's got a great groove and it's also got a very churchy feel to it.

STEFAN: It's is a little bit 'out there' going from playing *White House Blues*, *Sandwood Down To Kyle*, to *Little Niles*. It's a very wide spread of music. What's your feelings on this?

JOHN: The main ingredient of all of these pieces is that they have very strong melodies and the melodies are often not simply in a major key or a minor key but far more interesting. If you take these three supposedly different things – one an old-timey tune, another a jazz piece written in North Africa by a black American jazz musician and Sandwood *Down To Kyle* an actual strong modal song, very haunting and written by an English singer/songwriter in the north of Scotland,

White House Blues has got a really nice simple melody but it doesn't follow a set convention in the terms of it's notes. I'm attracted by melody and I'm attracted by what makes a melody strong and why it should work that way and often in my own taste it turns out that I'm attracted to tunes that are in one mode or another, earlier than major keys, earlier than minor keys. I think all these three tunes slip into that category, although *Little Niles* is far more jazzy in it's harmonies. It still has these ingredients – the A minor to D major the kind of dorian change that's very strong. The same thing happens in *White House Blues* . *Sandwood Down To Kyle* is different. It doesn't do that but it still has the same melodic qualities which I find attractive. Then I try to harmonize these pieces if they're a single line and then I find that I'm caught up in harmonizing something that was there before harmony as such was thought of. I find that I'm led into all kinds of avenues that appeal to me. I enjoy making arrangement that have got several lines rather than chords, then I find I need a tuning to play them in and then I wind up with a guitar arrangement.

STEFAN: You've studied music theory and the history of music. Is that helpful in your playing and how does it contribute to your arranging technique ?

JOHN: Well the amount of studying I did was to get me through my exams and very few tunes of this type were even involved in that kind of idea of harmonization, I was lucky that I had a music teacher early on who was very interested in early music but that was never part of the curriculum. I draw on everything I can as far as my own thinking process goes in making arrangements. I may have got a pretty stable base in academic harmony but I find that I don't use that as much but it's there. It's also an intuitive thing and really I'm open to a great many things. I'm intrigued by music that goes much further than even these ideas and these scales, for instance, if you were to listen to the pitches that were sung on some of the old folk recordings, the ones that were made by Percy Granger, you would find that not only are the singers not singing in a recognized scale, they weren't singing in a recognized mode and they weren't singing recognized pitches. Now when we play, we always tune when we're playing a fretted instrument. We're actually limited to what we consider to be a degree of intuneness but these old recordings didn't. They were in tune to themselves all the way through, rather like Rev. Gary Davis always tuned the guitar a little differently. It was the way he heard and the way he phrased. His sense of pitching. Well that's another avenue that's absolutely intriguing. As you know, I was just down at Jean Ritchie's house in Kentucky. She sings a lovely song which she wrote, where the actual quality of the major or minor third in the tune varies. This is really quite spellbinding. It throws most academics into a great tizz because it's either got to be one or the other. It can't be one and the other and something in between. That's where the fun starts.

STEFAN: Can you talk about how you set up your guitar, your right hand and how your guitar is set up?

JOHN: On playing the more complicated pieces with separate lines going at the same time, I like a guitar that's very evenly balanced or as close as I can get it. I don't really go for volume as much as evenness of overall sound. So I like something that I can hear clearly on the bass strings when I go up the neck beyond the seventh fret up -let's say to the 12th fret and beyond on the bass string. I like the strings to be of a fairly even gauged nature across when I play on stage because I tune down rather a lot. I use a .52 for my bass and because I like a rather stronger sound on the pickup that I use, I use a .12 for the top. These are very fine points but I mean if I were to play acoustically I think I would use a .50 for the bottom and maybe an .11 or .10 for the top. They're only slight differences but they do make a difference to the general feel of things. I find even small amounts like that are important. I find a .14 or .15 is fine for the 2nd and for the 3rd I use a covered .19 and 4th a covered .28 and for the 5th a covered .39.

STEFAN: What materials?

JOHN: I like the D'Darrio's nickel round wound strings. I actually like them because I prefer the sound of the nickel strings to the bronze strings. To my ears bronze strings have got a slightly thicker warmer sound and I prefer a thinner more defined sound especially if I'm playing pieces that have got lots of parts. I like low action.

STEFAN: And your right hand how is that setup?

JOHN: I usually play with my fingernails as I would have on a nylon string guitar and filed down and shaped them. I found that having to play professionally that was pretty hazardous. I use false nails stuck on underneath, ping-pong balls in fact, which are filed down and glued under, same as you would a box of player's nails. I've been experimenting with resin fingernails as well.

STEFAN; What is that?

JOHN: Pierre Bensusan has it done. It's what you get done in nail shops. It's a powder with a resin. You brush it on and build up a strong artificial nail. I find that the nails don't have to be particularly long and I've run into players that play really nicely and have shorter nails than me. That's maybe an idea – to roll the string off the flesh and then catch it with the nail. But I'm always intrigued by the way the nails wear down and the unusual places where the nails seem to wear. My nails seem to wear closer in to the tip of the finger than you imagine a string would hit and why that is I don't know. I think your hand position changes. I know I do a bit of teaching now and I've had classical players come in who have got an actual fixed right hand position that they have been taught and believe is the right position and everything else is wrong. I have to point out that the hand is on a wrist and you can move your hand to more or less any position and it still works. So I find when you're playing you need to drop the hand down to damp or you need to bring it right up to get just the nail sound and so on. I think this is all part of the playing and I think it happens now instinctively with myself and most players. So there isn't such a thing as a fixed right hand position.

The Birchmere Club, Maryland 1975   Photo by Jo Ayres

Judy

Standard Tuning, Capo 2

By John Renbourn ©1966 Logo Songs All Rights Reserved, Used With Permission

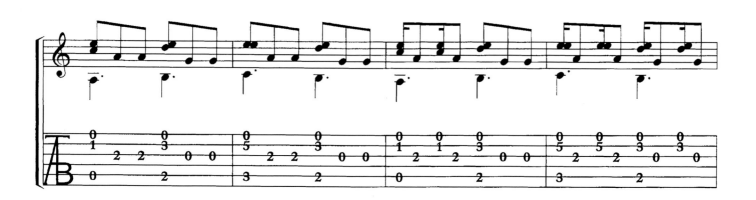

LINK PHRASE INTO ANJI

Anji

Standard Tuning, Capo 2

White House Blues

Standard Tuning

Buffalo   But   he   didn't   stay   too

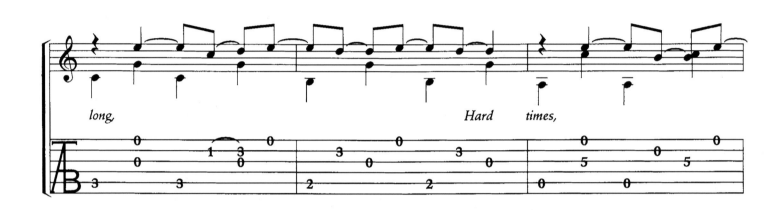

long,   Hard   times,

Hard   times,   Hard

times.

Mister McKinley, he didn't do no wrong
Just rode on down to Buffalo now, he didn't stay too long,
Hard times, hard times, hard times.

The people they came running 'round to see what had been done
You have shot the president down with your Ivor Johnson gun,
Hard times, hard times, hard times.

The train, yes the train, running on down the line,
Blowing at every station: McKinley is a-dying,
From Washington to Buffalo, hard times.

Roosevelt he's in the White House, he's doing his best,
McKinley he's in the graveyard now, a-taking of his rest.
Hard times, hard times, hard times.

I said, Roosevelt he's in the White House, drinking out of a silver cup,
And McKinley he's in the graveyard now, he'll never wake up,
Hard times, hard times, hard times.

Bottom Line, New York City, 1974   Photo by Herbert Grossman

Watch The Stars

Standard Tuning, Capo 2

run.   *Well   the   stars   run*

down   at   the   setting   of   the   sun,

Watch   the   stars,   See   how   they   run.

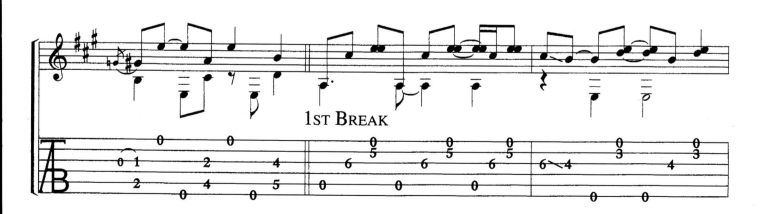

1ST BREAK

21

2ND BREAK

23

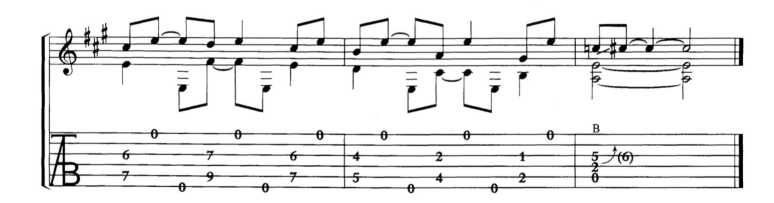

Watch the stars, see how they run,
Watch the stars, see how they run,
The stars run down at the setting of the sun,
Watch the stars, see how they run.

Watch the moon, see how it glows...
The moon sure glows when the sun goes down...

Watch the wind, see how it blows...
The wind's gonna blow when the sun goes down...

Lord Franklin

Standard Tuning

VERSE

Home - - - ward bound one night

on the deep, Swinging in my ham-

26

mock I fell a - sleep,

I dreamed a dream and thought it

true,

Concerning Franklin

27

and   his   gallant   crew.

Homeward bound one night on the deep,
Swinging in my hammock I fell asleep,
I dreamed a dream, and I thought it true,
Concerning Franklin, and his gallant crew.

With a hundred seamen he sailed away,
To the frozen ocean in the month of May,
To seek a passage around the pole,
Where we poor sailors do sometimes go.

Through cruel hardships they mainly strove,
Their ship on mountains of ice was drove,
Only the Eskimo, in his skin canoe,
Was the only one that ever came through.

In Baffin Bay where the whale fishes blow,
The fate of Franklin no man may know,
The fate of Franklin no tongue can tell,
Lord Franklin along with his seamen do dwell.

Now my burden, it gives me pain,
For my lost Franklin I would cross the main,
Ten thousand pounds would I freely give,
To say on earth, my Franklin do live.

28

My Sweet Potato

Dropped D Tuning: DADGBE

30

VARIATION 1

31

VARIATION 2

33

VARIATION 3

Different Turnaround —

VARIATION 4

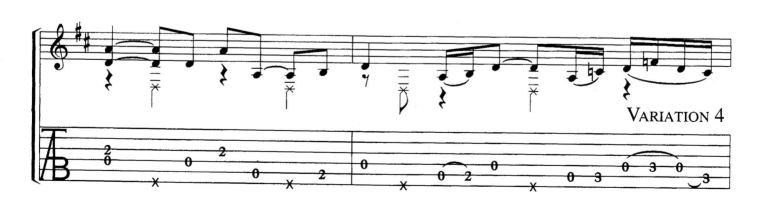

36

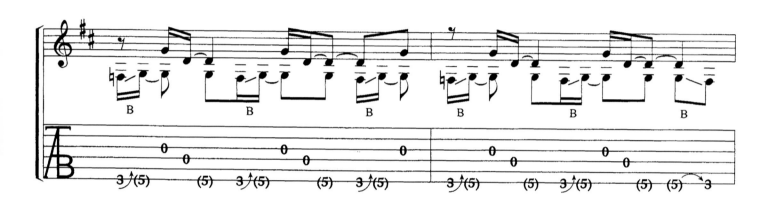

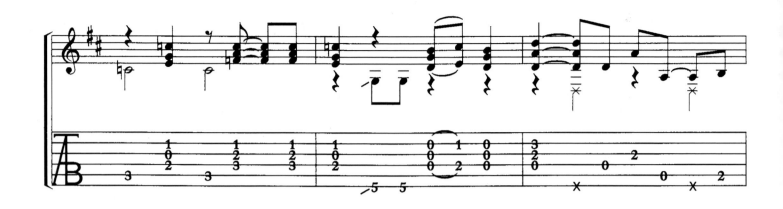

VARIATION 5

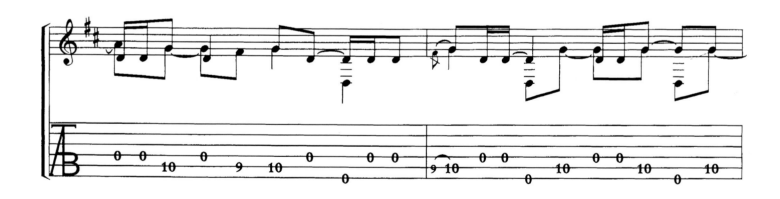

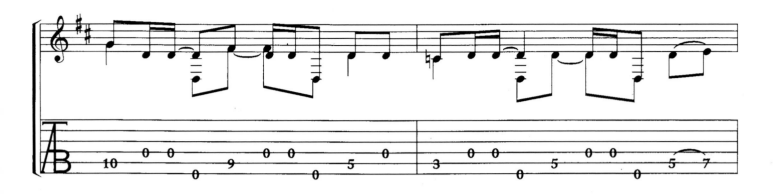

VARIATION 6

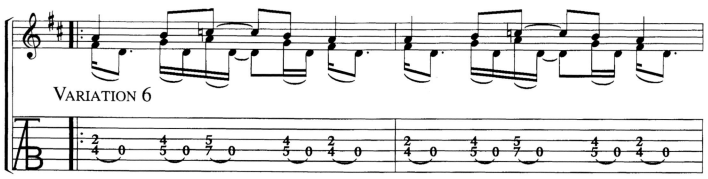

1.

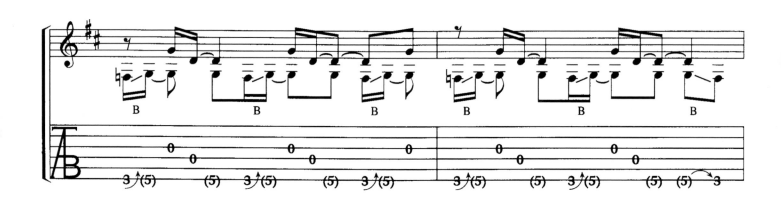
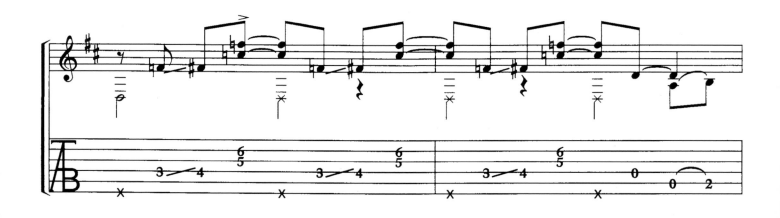
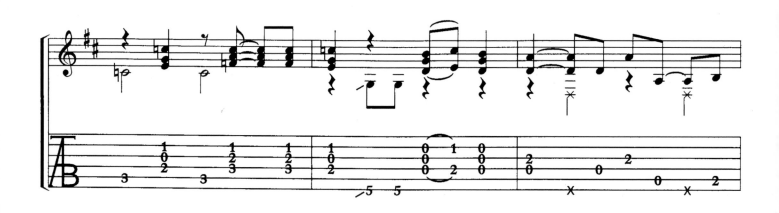

TAG

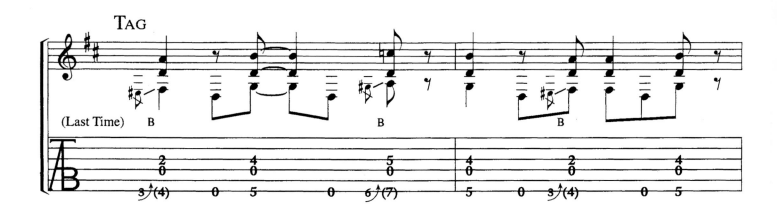

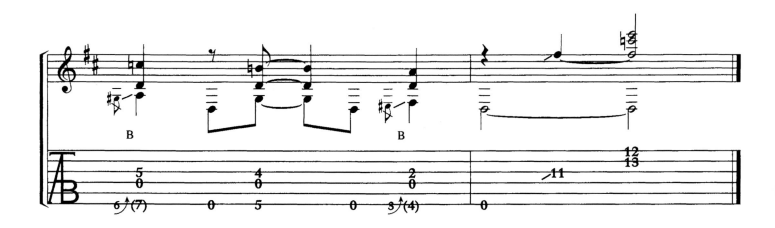

43

Abide With Me/Great Dreams From Heaven

Dropped D Tuning: DADGBE

44

VERSE

45

CHORUS

46

VARIATION 1

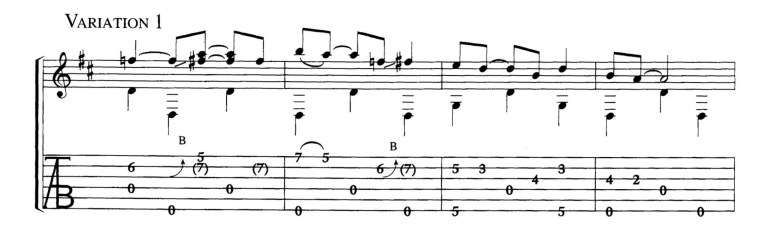

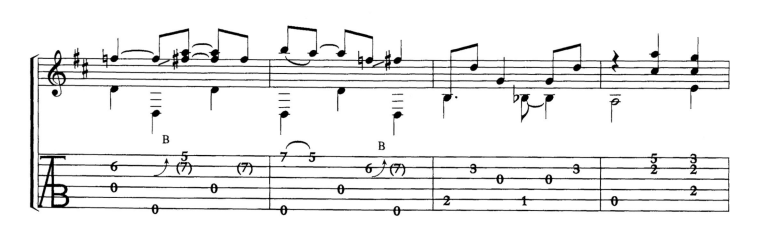

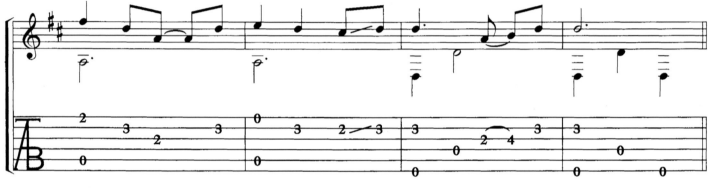

VARIATION 2

VARIATION 3

PATTERN IN SIXTHS

VARIATION

51

REPEAT VERSE AND CHORUS

FINAL ENDING OF CHORUS

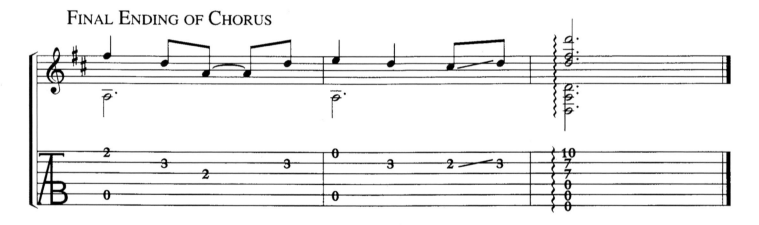

I had a great dream from heaven last night,
The angels in heaven are calling me home,
Thank God I can sing a song of His love,
I know someday I'll be singing above.
Why, it's glory to Jesus, save us from sin,
Glory to Jesus, I'm free, yes I am,
Thank God I can sing a song of His love,
I know someday I'll be singing above.

Now when mother and father forsake me, I know,
The angels…(as before)…

New York City, NY 1972

Photo by Herbert Grossman

The South Wind

Tuning: DADGBD

Trad. Arr. by John Renbourn ©1979 Pentangle Ltd. All Rights Reserved, Used With Permission

55

57

58

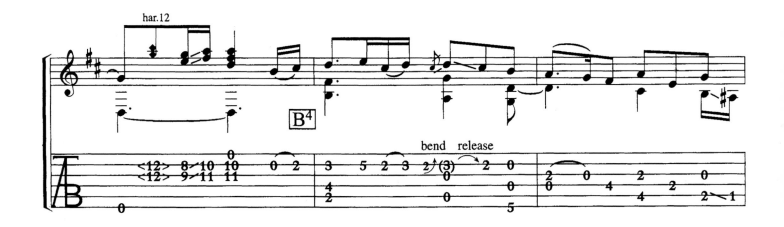

The Blarney Pilgrim

Tuning: DGDGBD, Capo 2

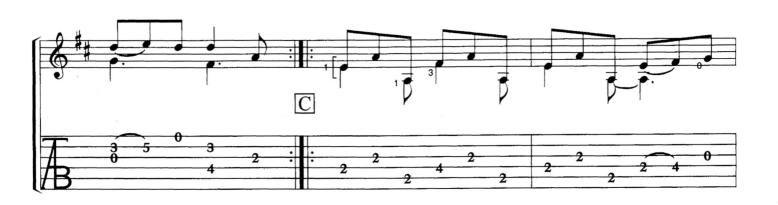

61

Bunyan's Hymn

Tuning: DGDGBD, Capo 3

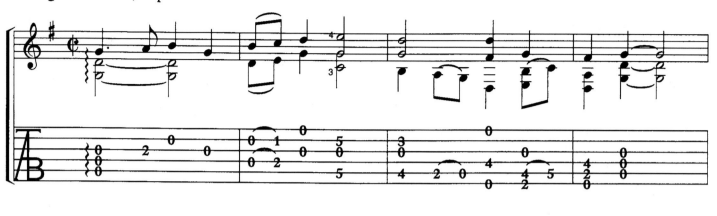

I Saw Three Ships

Tuning: DGDGBD, Capo 2

BRIDGE

(Repeat Bridge)

(Repeat Bridge)

The English Dance

Tuning: DGDGBD, Capo 2

VARIATION 2

70

REPEAT A C D E A.

ENDING

71

Lament For Owen Roe O'Neill

Tuning: DGDGB♭D

Trad. Arr. by John Renbourn ©1976 Pentangle Ltd. All Rights Reserved, Used With Permission

73

The Mist-Covered Mountains of Home

Tuning: DGDGB♭D, Capo 2

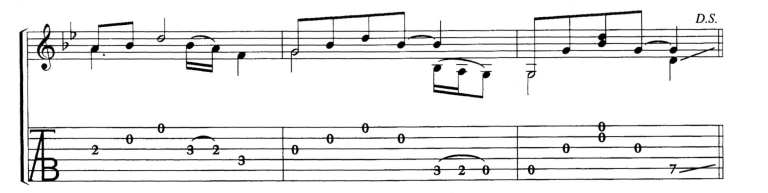

REPEAT $\boxed{A}$ ONCE, THEN $\boxed{B}$ ONCE.

Monte Porzio Catone, Italy 1977   Photo by Jo Ayres

The Orphan

Tuning: DGDGB♭D, Capo 2

Tramps and Hawkers

Tuning: DADGAD, Capo 4

Freely

Trad. Arr. by John Renbourn ©1979 Pentangle Ltd. All Rights Reserved, Used With Permission

To LINDSAY

81

Lindsay

Tuning: DADGAD, Capo 4

In tempo

Verse

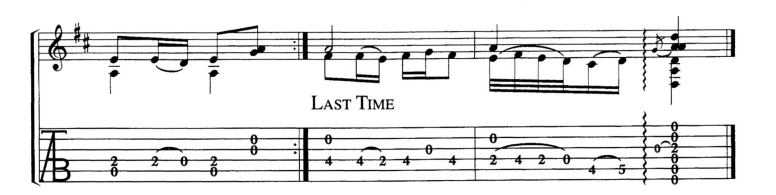

LAST TIME

Lindsay, he has ta'en to the road
Straight to the north he'll steer,
With a Speyside fiddle in his pack
Aye, he'll make a living, it's clear.

He's well met with a peddler drouth
And a chance to adjourn to the inn,
He's called for ale and he's ta'en up a fife,
And carelessly slipped to the tune.

Now all through the night they fiddled
        and fifed
For the dancers had ta'en to the floor,
They neither wanted a pipe nor a glass
Nor a lass when the music was o'er.

They played up through markets and fair
Till at length to the north they've come,
There they met black Janet the widow
Who sang as she rattled the drum

Now Lindsay's asked black Janet to dance,
And you've ne'er seen so bonny a pair,
She's ta'en him firm by the hand
And they skipped to the top of the stairs.

Here, she said, is a fine feather bed
Where a man, be he weary or drear,
May step for me a gay strathspey
With me lilting a tune in his ear.

Now Janet was as good as her word
And Lindsay has proven his worth;
May you all have so merry a dance
If ever you come to the north.

83

Sandwood Down To Kyle

Tuning: DADGAD

One Mon - day morn as I walked out___ the

wild birds for to see,___ I met a man___ up-on___

the road_____ and asked for char - i -

ty,   I met a man up - on the road_____

D.S. through Verses

_____ and asked for char - i - ty.

D.S. through Verses

PATTERN

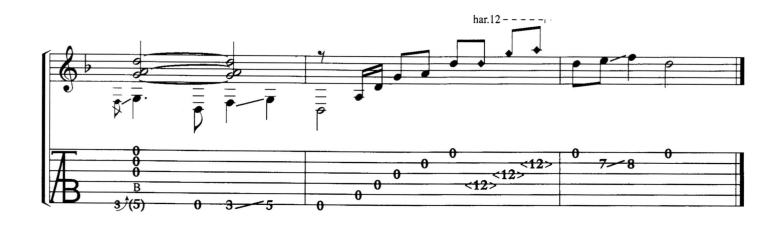

On Monday morn as I walked out, the wild birds for to see,
I met a man upon the road and asked for charity. (2x)

Come home with me and drink your fill, and comfort you shall find,
And tell me why you walk the road that leaves the hills behind.

For time has spent the summer, sir, and soon the leaves will fall,
I hear the sound within the wind that plays around your walls.

The bird must flee the winter, sir, she cannot stay behind,
To build her nest upon the snow; nor can I look for mine.

If I had a hundred homes, to live in, each a while,
I'd build them all along the coast, from Sandwood down to Kyle.

Stefan Grossman & John Renbourn, Monte Porzio, Italy 1978

Photo by Jo Ayres

Buffalo

Standard Tuning

2ND CHORUS

D.S. al Fine

John Renbourn & Stefan Grossman, Hadrian's Wall, England 1976

Photo by Jo Ayres

Transfusion

Standard Tuning

IMPROVISATION

My Dear Boy

Standard Tuning

99

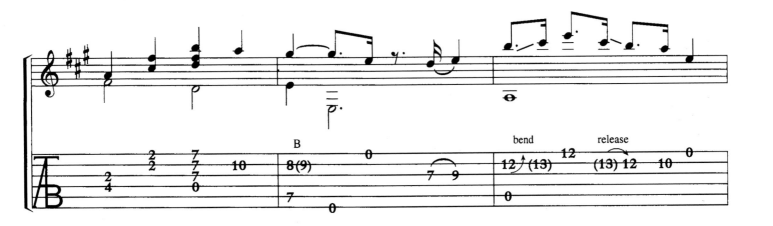

D.S. al Coda

CODA

Little Niles

Standard Tuning

D.S. 𝄋
(to 3rd ending)

105

IMPROV.

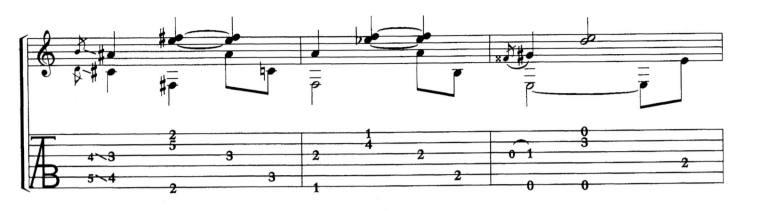

PLAY B, A, 3RD ENDING TO CODA

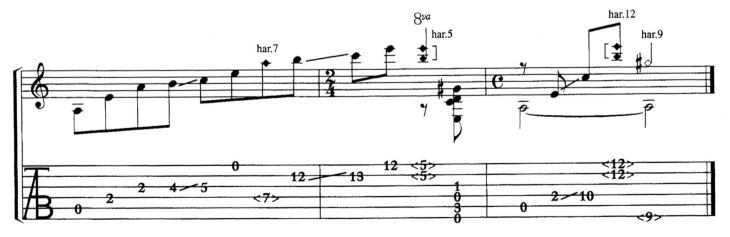

Cherry

Tuning: DGDGBE

111

To Coda ⊕

REPEAT [A]

[B²]   IMPROVISATION

113

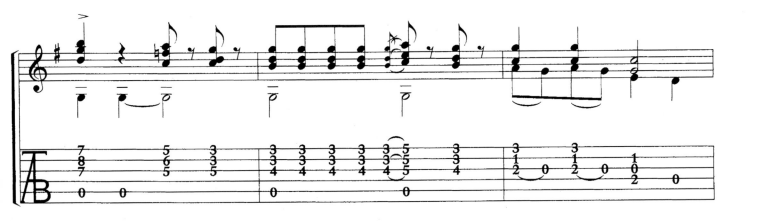

D.S. al Coda

CODA

118

New York City, 1975

Photo by Herbert Grossman

The Video Lessons of John Renbourn

(available from Stefan Grossman's Guitar Workshop, PO Box 802, Sparta, NJ 07871
Tel: 973 729 5544   Fax: 973 726 0568   Website: www.guitarvideos.com)

Folk, Blues & Beyond
Taught by John Renbourn

* *

78-min video • Level 2/3
56 page tab/music booklet
GW 907 $39.95

* *

In this lesson, John Renbourn presents a wide variety of fingerstyle arrangements from traditional ballads to country blues, from a Booker T. and the MG's rock instrumental to the church hymn *Abide With Me*. All receive the special touches of John's unique playing and are explained in detail with the help of split-screen video techniques that allow the student to clearly see and study what each hand is doing.
Titles include: *White House Blues, Judy, Anji, Watch The Stars, Lord Franklin, My Sweet Potato, Abide With Me* and *Great Dreams From Heaven.*

Celtic Melodies & Open Tunings
Taught by John Renbourn

* *

80-min video • Level 2/3
56 page tab/music booklet
GW 908 $39.95

* *

John Renbourn is well known for his recordings and performances of Celtic music. In this lesson he discusses and teaches his approach to arranging Celtic melodies using a wide variety of open tunings. All receive the special touches of John's playing and are explained in detail.
Titles include: *The South Wind, The Blarney Pilgrim, Bunyan's Hymn, I Saw Three Ships, The English Dance, Lament For Owen Roe O'Neill, Mist Covered Mountains Of Home, The Orphan, Lindsey* and *Sandwood Down To Kyle.*

Medieval & Renaissance Music For Fingerstyle Guitar
Taught by John Renbourn

* *

93-min video • Level 2/3
48 page tab/music booklet
GW 947 $39.95

* *

"For some time now I have periodically made transcriptions of early pieces mainly for my own enjoyment. My own interest in early music runs parallel to my interest in Western folk music. It was intriguing to consider the characteristics that are common in both. I discovered that even whole pieces, thought to exist only in manuscript, occasionally cropped up remarkably intact in current folk playing, and instruments long assumed silent were found to be still sounding in remote areas of Europe. I began by taking a medieval dance tune and treating it as I would a jig or reel, or drawing on contrapuntal practice in making arrangements of folk songs. In this video lesson I present five of these arrangements that I hope you will enjoy."
– John Renbourn
Titles include: *The Earle of Salisbury (standard tuning), Saltarello (DGDGCD tuning), Saltarello II (EAEF#AD tuning), Trotto (DGDGCD tuning)* and *Robin Is To The Greenwood Gone (standard tuning).*

The Jazz Tinge
Taught by John Renbourn

"Performer, composer, arranger, recording artist, teacher, schooled musician and improvisor. Precious few of the many fine guitarists currently plying their trade combine all of these attributes as successfully as John Renbourn. He has been working at his craft for over 30 years. As a performer he continues to tour the world. As a composer he has written some of the most technically brilliant and musically satisfying fingerstyle guitar pieces in the repertoire. His arranging skills for guitar are legendary, ranging from altered-tuning accompaniments of traditional folk songs, to Renaissance keyboard pieces to blues-infected jazz."
– FINGERSTYLE GUITAR

* *

80-min video • Level 3/4
48 page tab/music booklet
GW 917 $39.95

* *

THE JAZZ TINGE presents five exciting and challenging jazz compositions that each receive John's unique and exciting fingerstyle approach. The compositions of Chico Hamilton Randy Weston, Dollar Brand and John's own original instrumentals are discussed in detail. Split-screen video techniques are used, allowing the student to clearly see and study what each hand is doing. This lesson is for intermediate and advanced students.
Titles include: *Buffalo, Transfusion, My Dear Boy, Little Niles* and *Cherry.*

120